BIRDS

PREDATORS

Lynn M. Stone

Rourke Publications, Inc.
Vero Beach, Florida 32964

Edited by Sandra A. Robinson

PHOTO CREDITS
All photos © Lynn M. Stone

Library of Congress Cataloging-in-Publication Data

Stone, Lynn M.
  Birds / by Lynn Stone.
     p. cm. — (Predators)
  Includes index.
  Summary: Discusses the physical characteristics and behavior
of hawks, eagles, owls, and other kinds of birds of prey.
  ISBN 0-86625-440-4
  1. Birds of prey—North America—Juvenile literature. [1. Birds of
prey. 2. Predatory animals.] I. Title. II. Series: Stone, Lynn M.
Predators.
QL696.F3S75   1993
598—dc20
                                        92-34485
                                           CIP
                                           AC

TABLE OF CONTENTS

BIRDS AS PREDATORS

Some of the largest and most beautiful birds in North America are killers. Even America's national bird, the bald eagle, is a skillful killer.

However, the eagle kills for a good reason. Like all **predators,** or hunting animals, it kills other animals—its **prey**—for its own survival. Predators live by eating the flesh of their prey.

Bird predators are found in many different kinds of places. Almost every type of natural area is a home, or **habitat,** for one feathered predator or another.

America's national bird, the bald eagle is a skillful predator

BIRD WEAPONS

Birds that hunt use their feet, beaks or both to capture and kill prey.

Hawks, eagles and owls are the especially fine hunters known as **birds of prey.** They have sharp claws, or **talons,** to kill prey. They also have sharp, hooked beaks to tear flesh. About 50 **species,** or kinds, of hawks, eagles and owls live in the United States and Canada.

America's other hunting birds lack talons, but they use their beaks as weapons. **Herons** stab, **cormorants** grab, and pelicans trap their prey.

6

Birds of prey kill with sharp talons and tear flesh with sharp, hooked beaks

HOW BIRDS HUNT

North American birds have an advantage over other predators—the ability to fly. If one hunting area is poor, they can fly to another.

For birds of prey, flying is also the means to quickly attack prey in the air, on the ground or in the water.

Herons stalk—walk carefully toward—their prey, and then stab it with their long, sharp beaks. The tall cranes walk along using their long bills to pluck spiders, little fish, frogs and snakes.

Cormorants are among the birds that chase fish underwater and grab them in their beaks.

Young sandhill crane in a wet meadow feeds on a ribbon snake

BIRDS OF PREY

The most widely-known bird predators are the birds of prey—hawks, eagles and owls. They are generally large birds, and they often tackle animals that are almost as big as they are.

Birds of prey swoop or dive from the air to attack. Their downward flights are remarkably fast, and their strong, hooklike talons are deadly.

Birds of prey eat other birds, snakes, fish, muskrats, rabbits, mice, and almost any animal they can surprise and overpower.

Bald eagle's flight, guided by excellent vision, is remarkably fast

A cormorant dries its feathers after an underwater hunt

Roseate spoonbills trap little animals in sensitive, spoon-shaped bills

HAWKS AND EAGLES

Hawks and eagles are the daylight birds of prey. They have extremely good vision. They can locate prey that's a great distance away.

Most hawk and eagle attacks are on land. However, the bald eagle and osprey, or fish hawk, are terrific fishermen. They use their talons to snag fish swimming near the water's surface.

A group of sharp-winged hawks known as falcons are skilled at using their talons to strike and kill other birds in mid-air!

An osprey (fish hawk) brings a flounder to its feeding perch

OWLS

Many of the prey animals that escaped hawks during the day become owl prey at night.

Owls are silent **nocturnal,** or nighttime, hunters. Special feathers quiet the normal flapping sound of feathers in flight, so owls strike their prey with complete surprise.

Although even owls cannot see in complete darkness, their vision in low light is the best of any animal. Owls also have extremely keen hearing. The tiny squeak or footstep of a mouse on leaves will alert an owl 75 feet away.

*A screech owl prepares
to dine on a nighttime snack*

FISHERMEN WITH FEATHERS

Feathered fishermen fill their bellies using an assortment of hunting styles. None is more spectacular than the brown pelican's head-first dive into the ocean. The pelican's pouch, attached to its throat and bill, traps fish like a big bowl.

The long-necked **anhinga,** or snakebird, swims underwater and spears fish with its bill. The **spoonbill** catches fish and other little animals that it slurps into a sensitive, paddle-shaped bill.

The wood stork drags its lower bill in shallow, muddy water. The bill slams shut when it bumps a small fish.

A brown pelican, eyes on a fish target, dives toward the sea

BIRDS AND THEIR ENEMIES

Not too many years ago, birds of prey were commonly shot. Often, it was just because they were easy targets.

Thousands more birds of prey died from eating animals that had DDT, a poison, in their bodies. DDT was used in large amounts to kill insects.

Several kinds of fishing birds—herons and **egrets** especially—were nearly wiped out 100 years ago. Their long, lacy feathers were in great demand for women's hats.

The destruction of good wildlife habitats also reduced the numbers of birds.

Egrets and other wading birds were once slaughtered for their lacy feathers

SAVING BIRDS THAT HUNT

People enjoy birds. Their welfare is more important to people than it once was.

Birds of prey are protected by strict laws in North America, as are the birds that fish. It is hoped feathered hats will never be popular again.

The birds themselves are protected. Now, it is just as important to protect their food supply and living space. It does no good to protect an eagle if it has no fish to eat and no tree in which to nest.

Glossary

anhinga (an HIN guh) — large, blackish diving bird with daggerlike beak and webbed feet

birds of prey (BIRDS uhv PRAY) — the hawks, eagles, vultures and owls; birds with talons and hooked beaks which feed on other animals

cormorant (KOR mor ant) — large, dark diving bird with slightly hooked beak and webbed feet

egret (E greht) — one of a group of long-legged wading birds with sharp bills and, in most species, white feathers

habitat (HAB uh tat) — the kind of place in which an animal lives, such as forest

heron (HAIR un) — any one of several long-legged wading birds with long, sharp bills

nocturnal (nok TUR nul) — more active at night than in daylight

predator (PRED a tor) — an animal that kills another animal for food

prey (PRAY) — an animal or animals that are hunted for food by another animal

species (SPEE sheez) — within a group of closely related animals, such as eagles, one certain kind or type (*bald* eagle)

spoonbill (SPOON bill) — a long-legged wading bird with an unusual, spoon-shaped bill and pink feathers (roseate spoonbill)

talons (TAL unz) — long, hooked claws on the feet of birds of prey

INDEX